THE PENOBSCOT

KATHERINE M. DOHERTY AND CRAIG A. DOHERTY

THE PENOBSCOT

Franklin Watts   A Division of Grolier Publishing
New York   London   Hong Kong   Sydney   Danbury, Connecticut
A First Book

Map by Joe LeMonnier
Cover photograph copyright ©: Ben Klaffke
Photographs copyright ©: Ben Klaffke: pp. 3, 8, 19, 28, 38, 40, 45, 51, 57; The
Bettmann Archive: pp. 13, 30; North Wind Picture Archives: pp. 14, 23;
Collections of the Bangor Historical Society: p. 17; UPI/Bettmann: pp. 21, 48;
Frank Speck/University of Pennsylvania Museum, Philadelphia: pp. 26
(S4–139110), 32 (S4–139112), 36 (NC35–13964), 52 (S4–139083); The Abbe
Museum, Bar Harbor, Maine: pp. 34, 42; The Jimmy Carter Library, National
Archives: p. 55.

Library of Congress Cataloging-in-Publication Data
Doherty, Katherine M.
The Penobscot / by Katherine M. Doherty and Craig A. Doherty.
p. cm. — (A First book)
Includes bibliographical references and index.
ISBN 0-531-20207-0
1. Penobscot Indians—Juvenile literature.   I. Doherty, Craig A.
II. Title. III. Series.
E99.P5D65   1995
974.1'004973—dc20   95-11291 CIP AC

CONTENTS

To our families

PENOBSCOT HOMELAND

Some twelve thousand years ago, a large group of American Indian tribes known as Eastern Woodland Indians lived in the deep woodlands of eastern and northern America. They depended on surrounding forests for their survival. The earliest American Indians in the Northeast were hunters and gatherers, moving according to the season and availability of food.

As time passed, almost all American Indians took up some form of *agriculture*. This allowed them to settle in one area and form separate groups. One group of Eastern Woodland Indians, the Penobscot (pronounced puh-NOB-scot), which means "the rocky place," settled in what is known today as the state of Maine.

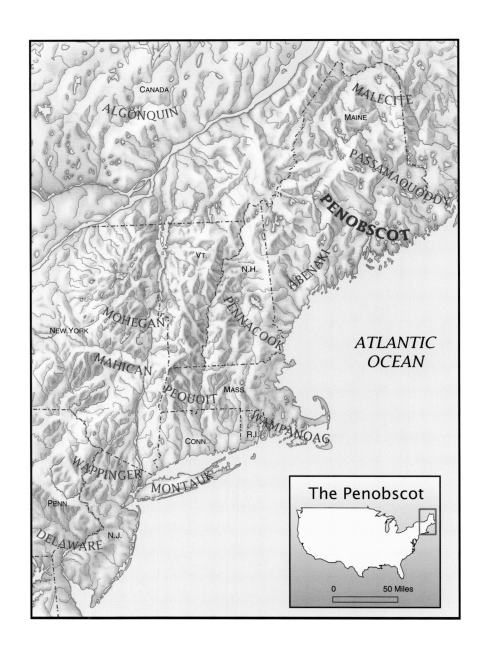

CANADA

ALGONQUIN

MALECITE

MAINE

PASSAMAQUODDY

PENOBSCOT

VT.

N.H.

ABENAKI

MOHEGAN

NEW YORK

PENNACOOK

ATLANTIC OCEAN

MAHICAN

PEQUOIT

MASS

WAMPANOAG

CONN.

R.I.

WAPPINGER

MONTAUK

PENN.

N.J.

DELAWARE

The Penobscot

0   50 Miles

Many Indian groups were linked by common languages. The Penobscot language belongs to the *Algonquian language* group. The Penobscot speak Eastern Abenaki and are considered an Abenaki tribe. Most of the other tribes in Maine and the Canadian coastal provinces, the Passamaquoddy and the Abenaki, for example, also spoke Abenaki dialects.

The traditional homeland of the Penobscot Indians includes the land around the Penobscot River, the longest river in the state of Maine, and Penobscot Bay, which it runs into. It is believed that the ancestors of the Penobscot first began living in this area about nine thousand years ago. *Artifacts* found on the present-day Penobscot Reservation indicate that the Penobscot are one of the few tribes in North America to have inhabited the same territory for so long.

The Penobscot did not believe in individual ownership of property; however, their territory was carefully divided. In the interior of the woodlands, each Penobscot village had specific hunting areas. These areas were further divided into smaller areas for each family, where they hunted and gathered the wild foods that were essential to their survival in the woodlands.

THE COMING OF THE EUROPEANS

Before Europeans first came to the coast of Maine, in the 1400s, approximately forty thousand American Indians were living in the present state of Maine, ten thousand of whom were members of the Penobscot tribe. By 1800, that population of ten thousand was reduced to only about two hundred.

The earliest explorers in the area, Europeans such as Giovanni da Verrazano, Samuel de Champlain, and others, often wrote of stopping at the Penobscot River. Despite early visits, the Europeans were slow to colonize this region. However, between 1617 and 1619, the Penobscot were stricken with a smallpox plague that spread throughout northeastern North America. Some estimate that as much as two thirds of the American Indian population of the area was

FRENCH EXPLORER SAMUEL DE CHAMPLAIN
WAS ONE OF THE FIRST EUROPEANS TO COME
TO NEW ENGLAND IN THE EARLY 1600s.

THE ARRIVAL OF THE EUROPEAN COLONISTS
CHANGED THE PEACEFUL LIVES OF PENOBSCOT
COMMUNITIES FOREVER.

wiped out by smallpox, a disease that was often fatal to the Indians. Unlike the Europeans, who had brought this disease to the Americas, the Indians had never been exposed to it and therefore had no immunity, or resistance to the germ.

As more Europeans arrived from various countries, conflicts over land followed. France and England struggled for control of North America and its vast lands and natural resources. During this time, the Penobscot participated in or were affected by eight wars, including the American Revolution. By the end of the Revolution only a few hundred Penobscot were left, trying desperately to hold on to their lands and culture. All but one of the villages of the Penobscot were abandoned. The surviving members of the tribe moved to a village on Indian Island, a part of the current reservation in Old Town, Maine.

The Penobscot lifestyle and culture had already been greatly affected by European contact. Even before any settlers arrived, fur traders were active in Maine. The Penobscot quickly turned from their hunting and agricultural lifestyle to trading furs for European manufactured goods.

By this time, the Penobscot lost their expansive lands in the interior of Maine to the Europeans. In 1796 the government of Massachusetts, of which Maine was then a part, took 200,000 acres (80,900 ha) from the Penobscot by "treaty." The treaty called for Massachusetts to give the Penobscot cloth, blankets, shot and powder for guns, food, and other items each year in exchange for the property. In 1818, the colonial government forced the Penobscot to give up almost all their remaining lands. They were allowed to keep four townships and the islands on which they lived in the Penobscot River. In 1833, the Penobscot were cheated out of the four remaining townships on the mainland and were left in poverty on their islands.

During the nineteenth century, some of the remaining members of the Penobscot tribe acted as guides for travelers unfamiliar with the region. Henry David Thoreau, the author most famous for his book *Walden*, was led by Penobscot guides on his journeys through the Maine wilderness. Other Penobscot worked harvesting the trees of their former lands for the white man's growing lumber industry. The Penobscot were best known in the lumber business for the hard and dangerous work they did driving logs down the Penobscot River.

THIS DETAILED PENOBSCOT INDIAN CHURCH
CALENDAR WAS MADE BY THE GUIDE WHO TOOK
HENRY DAVID THOREAU THROUGH MAINE.

FAMILY BANDS AND VILLAGES

The organization of Penobscot society depended on family relations. Family bands of the Penobscot were arranged according to a child's father's family. Each family was led by a male member. This leader was called the *sagamore*, which means "strong man" in the language of the Penobscot. Each group or band was known by an animal name. Bear, Rabbit, Wildcat, Raven, and even Lobster were some of the animal names associated with family groups. At the beginning of the twentieth century there were twenty-two family bands, each with its own animal symbol.

The survival of these family groups depended on the cooperation of all the members of the band. Each family had a clearly defined territory in the interior. This territory was used for hunting animals and gath-

THIS CARVING OF A BEAVER IS ONE PENOBSCOT
FAMILY'S SYMBOL.

ering other resources. Families respected the boundaries of the territories. Trespassers feared the power of a group's *shaman*, the spiritual leader of a band, and would obtain permission to travel through another band's territory if the need arose.

In earlier times, the sagamore was probably a position of respect more than one of power. The sagamores were responsible for settling disputes among members of their band and representing the band at large ceremonies. Later, when the tribe had to send a single leader to negotiate with the European settlers, the position became important.

The Penobscot considered the entire Penobscot River valley their territory, but their permanent villages were located near the mouth of the river. These villages, like the land in the interior, were organized according to family bands.

OLDER MEMBERS OF PENOBSCOT VILLAGES
COMMAND SPECIAL RESPECT.

RELIGION AND BELIEFS

The Penobscot believe that a creator spirit made the lands of the Penobscot and all of its creatures, including humans. This creator spirit, called *Glooskap*, first created tiny spirits that lived in the rocks. Those spirits in turn created all the plants and animals. The Penobscot believe that Glooskap then made people by shooting at trees with his bow and that the first Penobscot people came out of the bark of an ash tree.

The Penobscot also believe that this creator spirit Glooskap had to remake some of his animals because they were too big and threatened the survival of the Penobscot people. Some of the other animals that might have threatened people were sent north, away from where people lived. For example, the Penobscot

THE PENOBSCOT, LIKE OTHER INDIAN TRIBES,
HONOR ANIMAL SPIRITS.

believe that after Glooskap created polar bears, he sent them north, where they could not harm anyone.

The traditional belief among the Penobscot is that every aspect of their lives, and of their existence, is closely connected to the spirit world. For example, their success when they went out hunting or fishing came from the spirits of the animals, which allowed them to succeed. Because the Penobscot depended on good hunting and gathering to survive, they were very respectful of the spirit world.

The Penobscot were led in their spiritual activities by shamans. The shaman was a spiritually knowledgeable and powerful person who knew all the important religious tribal rituals and practices. A shaman might also have skill as a healer and prophet.

DAILY LIFE

Childhood and Education ➙ Life for an infant among the Penobscot could be very difficult. The winters in Maine were frequently severe. Babies born in the late fall or winter often would not survive to see spring. Children who made it through their first winter were highly valued by family bands. After all, the strength of the band depended on its ability to grow and prosper.

Like many American Indians, the Penobscot used cradleboards to carry their infants. The baby was bound into the wooden board, which was strapped to the mother's back or placed upright on the floor. Cradleboards are approximately 1 foot (30 cm) wide and 2 to 3 feet (60 to 90 cm) long. The Penobscot

A PENOBSCOT WOMAN FROM THE EARLY 1900s
SECURES HER CHILD IN A HAMMOCK HANGING
FROM TWO TREES.

cradleboards were often decorated with carvings and cutouts. Many consider the Penobscot cradleboards among the finest made. When children were not attached to their cradleboards, they were often placed in baby-size hammocks made from buckskin. A Penobscot mother could hang a hammock up indoors or outside, depending on her activity and the weather.

Traditionally, Penobscot children began to help the adult members of their bands with the daily chores, such as finding and preparing food, as soon as they were able. They watched and worked with their elders to learn. By observing and then participating, Penobscot children received their education. They also learned about the traditions of their family and tribe from the adults who told tales at night, especially in the winter when the people spent more time indoors.

From a very young age, children were taught to be quiet. This quality was important to the Penobscot. Loud activities scared game away and might also alert enemies in the area. Although Penobscot children were allowed to play, it was very different from the way children play today. Because they had to help in the hunting, fishing, and gathering activities of the band, their games reflected the work they were expected to learn and perform as they matured.

CORNHUSK DOLLS WERE A FAVORITE OF YOUNG AND OLD
ALIKE; THE YOUNG PLAYED WITH THEM, AND THE OLD TOLD
TALES ABOUT THEM. THEY ARE WITHOUT FACES BECAUSE IT
WAS BELIEVED THAT WITH A FACE THE DOLL MIGHT
CAPTURE A SOUL AND TURN INTO A REAL PERSON.

Farming and Gathering ➤ The climate where the Penobscot lived made it difficult for them to grow crops. Some years the weather caused their crops of corn, beans, and squash to fail or the harvests to be very small. This difficulty prevented the Penobscot from becoming full-time farmers. It forced them to continue to depend more on hunting and gathering than the Woodland tribes who lived in warmer climates.

Fortunately, the woods, lakes, rivers, and bays of their territory were rich in food resources. Raspberries, blueberries, wild grapes, and cherries all grew in abundance. The Penobscot ate all these fruits fresh when they were in season and also dried them to eat in the winter. Young members of the group often did much of the gathering. Gathering food was a social occasion as well as a practical activity.

The Penobscot burned areas on the islands in the bay and river to encourage the growth of berries. They also gathered nuts and other wild plants. Groundnuts were especially important to the Penobscot. The groundnut is not really a nut but an edible root similar to a potato.

The Penobscot also collected sap from maple trees. They did not have metal pots to boil their sap in. Instead, they boiled the sap liquid by placing hot rocks in wooden and bark containers. Using this

COLLECTING AND PREPARING THE SAP THAT FLOWED
FROM LOCAL MAPLE TREES WAS BOTH A SOCIAL AND
PRODUCTIVE ACTIVITY FOR THE PENOBSCOT.

technique, the Penobscot were able to reduce the sap to sweet syrup or sugar.

Fishing → In the spring, when numerous fish swam upstream to *spawn*, the Penobscot left the woods and moved to camps along the bay and river. During the spawning runs of shad, alewife, salmon, eels, and sturgeon, it was easy to catch plenty of fish. The Penobscot caught fish in many ways.

One tool the Penobscot used during the spawning runs was a large *dip net* attached to a 10-foot(3-m)-long pole. Salmon and shad were often caught this way. Most of the fish caught in the spring were dried or smoked for preservation and storage.

The Penobscot also built fish *weirs* in the rivers and streams. A fish weir is a fence of sticks and brush that forces fish to swim into a narrow opening, where they can be easily scooped up with a net or speared as they swim through. In the Penobscot River, the weirs jutted out from the bank and forced the fish toward shore. In smaller streams, the weir crossed the entire stream.

The Penobscot also used hooks and lines to fish. Sometimes they used unbaited bone hooks and flat stones as jigs, or fishing devices, that they lowered to the bottom of the water and "jiggled" up and down

A PENOBSCOT MAN USES A SPEAR TO CATCH
FISH FROM THE SHORE.

to attract fish. Fishing with jigs was usually done in the bay, where large schools of pollack and other fish could be found feeding.

Other times, the Penobscot used baited hooks. They also developed weighted lures that could be cast with a hand line. A stone that had been covered with the white *tallow*, or hard fat, from a deer to attract the fish was used as the weight. A hook, traditionally made from the breastbone of a bird, was attached below the stone.

On some occasions, the Penobscot used poisonous plants to catch fish. When the water was low, in late summer, they put a mixture of pokeberries and other plants in the water of a stream. Within an hour, dead and dying eels floated to the surface. Children were in charge of gathering them up. Then, the women skinned, salted, and hung the eels on branches to dry.

The Penobscot used harpoons to kill large fish and sea mammals. They fished for sturgeon at night, using torches to attract them to the surface. They used harpoons to catch porpoises as well. Porpoise hunting was the most dangerous; to catch them, the Penobscot had to take their canoes out into the open ocean. They hunted the porpoise for its fat, which was used for cooking.

THESE BARBED FISHING HARPOONS MADE OF BONE WERE
FOUND IN FRENCHMAN BAY, NOT FAR FROM PENOBSCOT BAY,
AND ARE ROUGHLY TWO THOUSAND YEARS OLD.

Shellfish were another important food source. The Penobscot went to the mud flats of the bay to gather large quantities of clams, which were dried every summer to eat during the long winter. They went out in their canoes to spear lobsters and crabs in the shallows of the bay.

Hunting ➡ The Penobscot hunted moose, deer, caribou, bears, beavers, rabbits, and many other animals. These animals provided meat as well as hides to make clothing and bedding, and bones and antlers to make tools. The Penobscot wasted little from their hunts. They even used the beaver's long, sharp front teeth as blades for small knives.

Hunting was a vital part of Penobscot life. During the hunting season, the entire band moved inland. The vast lands that make up the Penobscot River drainage were divided among the different bands so that everyone had ample hunting territory. Natural landmarks—mountains, hills, rivers, and streams—that were familiar to all separated these territories.

The work that had to be done during the hunting season was clearly divided between males and females. Girls learned the skills needed to preserve and prepare the meat, hides, and other useful parts of the animals. The boys learned the skills of the hunter.

DURING THE BUSY HUNTING SEASON, THE YOUNG LEARN FROM THE OLD. IN THIS HISTORIC PHOTOGRAPH, A PENOBSCOT BOY AND AN EXPERIENCED HUNTER TRAVEL TOGETHER ON SNOWSHOES.

At busy times, the men and boys would help with the butchering.

One traditional hunting ritual was the sharing of any killed animals. When a boy made his first kill, he gave away all the meat and ate none himself. It was believed that if a boy kept his first kill for himself the spirits would never let him be a successful hunter again. The first animal killed by any hunter during the fall hunt was also given away to assure his luck for the rest of the season.

A select group of young hunters lived apart from the rest of the community and remained unmarried. These hunters were called runners because they could run down a deer in the forest. A runner lost his status when a younger man could outrun him and took his place.

Most Penobscot hunters were more conventional in their hunting methods, using bows and arrows, lances, and knives. Moose, which were plentiful in the hunting territories, were the most important prey.

Among the Europeans, the Penobscot were well known for their moose calls. During the autumn mating season of the moose, the females call the males. The Penobscot were able to imitate these calls by blowing or grunting into cone-shaped *birch bark* horns, which amplified the sound. The bull moose responded to the call and investigated its source,

PENOBSCOT HUNTERS USED BIRCH BARK HORNS
LIKE THIS ONE TO MAKE LOUD MOOSE CALLS,
WHICH DREW THE MOOSE NEAR.

allowing the hunter a very close and easy shot. Sometimes the hunters made their moose calls from canoes and waited for the moose to appear on the bank of the river or stream. The Penobscot also hunted moose in the winter when the moose could not travel easily in the deep snow and the hunters, wearing snowshoes, could sneak up on the moose.

Everyone, including the women and children, helped in the preparation of the animals taken in the hunt. They butchered and dried the meat and prepared the skin for tanning. The younger boys were encouraged to pursue smaller game with their bows so they could learn the skills needed to be good hunters in the future.

The Penobscot hunted deer in many ways. In the fall, they stalked their prey, sneaking up quietly on the hunted animal. When the snows came, the deer would *yard up* for the winter. Yarding up is a survival tactic for deer. A large group of deer will gather together in a dense growth of softwood trees. The herd packs down the deep snow so that the animals can move about and eat the needles and buds off the lower branches of the trees. The Penobscot hunters used the behavior of the deer to their advantage. After the deer beat down trails in and around these yards, the hunters would use the paths through the snow to ambush deer or snare them in traps.

THE PENOBSCOT PREPARED THE SKIN OF
AN ANIMAL FOR TANNING BY REMOVING THE
FUR WITH A BONE SCRAPER.

After the arrival of the European fur traders, the hunting of animals with valuable fur increased. The traders wanted beaver, mink, ermine, and fox furs for the clothing markets in Europe. They also brought new technology and goods from Europe, and the Penobscot quickly adapted to use them. Metal cooking utensils, knives, axes, and eventually guns replaced traditional tools. The fur trade caused the depletion of many species of animals—and food sources for American Indians—in the woods of Maine and throughout North America.

Shelter ➤ The type of shelter used by the Penobscot depended on how long they planned to stay at a certain place and what time of year it was. Their sturdiest shelters were built for winter use and were of two basic shapes—cone shaped (like a tepee) or square.

Both shapes were built in the same way. A center pole 10 to 12 feet (3 to 3.7 m) tall was set on a flat stone. The stone protected the pole from fire and provided a solid foundation. Longer poles were then lashed to the center pole. One unique feature of the Penobscot structure was a wooden hoop. This hoop was placed about halfway up the poles. It gave strength to the shelter frame and was a handy place to hang clothes and personal items.

THIS MODEL OF A PENOBSCOT SHELTER IS COVERED
WITH BIRCH TREE BARK AND STITCHED TOGETHER.

The Penobscot used two types of outer covering for their shelters—branches (from spruce, hemlock, and balsam trees) or birch bark. The branches were layered over the frame. When birch bark was used, large sheets of it were sewn together with spruce roots. As many as three layers of bark were used.

The shelters had a smoke hole in the center of the roof to allow smoke from the fire inside the shelter to escape. Inside the shelter, the Penobscot laid logs to divide the cooking space from the sleeping space, where spruce branches covered with furs served as beds. Most shelters had two small doors. On cold nights or when the weather was bad, the smoke hole and the doors were covered with deer or moose skins.

During the coldest nights, the Penobscot built large fires outside the shelter and piled rocks on them. When the rocks were hot, they put them back in the shelter to provide heat for the night. They also covered the inside walls of the shelters with animal hides for insulation.

The Penobscot sometimes built small log houses with tree branch or bark roofs. It is unclear whether this kind of shelter was a traditional Penobscot building or an adaptation of the houses that the earliest European settlers in the area built.

In the warm months when the Penobscot were traveling to fishing and hunting camps, they built temporary lean-to shelters. A lean-to has one flat roof that slopes down from a cross pole. The Penobscot either suspended the cross pole between two trees or set it on forked poles stuck into the ground. Then, they leaned poles against the cross pole to form the roof and covered the roof with branches or bark. The high end of the lean-to faced the cooking fire and was left open. Depending on the season and the weather, the sides were left open or covered. Spruce branches were placed on the floor of the lean-to and covered with furs for sleeping.

When the Penobscot picked a site for a camp or village, they had four main requirements—good drinking water, an ample supply of firewood, easy access to and from the site by canoe, and a location that was hidden or defensible against enemies. There was no specific arrangement to the Penobscot camps and villages. The sagamore picked the spot for his shelter first and then the rest of the group built their shelters somewhere near that dwelling.

Traditional Foods ➡ The staples of the traditional Penobscot diet were meat and fish. The Penobscot ate meat fresh, roasted over an open fire or added to stews. Any surplus meat was cut into strips and

LOBSTERS, FISH, AND CLAMS WERE STAPLES OF
TRADITIONAL PENOBSCOT FARE.

smoked over a fire to preserve it for later. Fish was also cooked and eaten fresh as well as dried and smoked for later consumption. The Penobscot also had their own version of a clambake.

The Penobscot prepared a clambake by building a pile of wood and stones in alternating layers. When the pile was big enough, they started the fire. When the wood had burned down, a pile of very hot rocks remained. The food, which included many kinds of shellfish and corn, was placed on the hot rocks and covered with seaweed. The food took about an hour to cook.

The Penobscot made most of their cooking utensils out of wood or bark. They created birch bark bowls by sewing birch bark together with spruce or cedar roots and sealing the seams with pitch from tree sap. They made large and heavy pottery out of clay with ground clamshells, added to strengthen the pots.

The staple of Penobscot stews or soups were corn and beans. The rest of the ingredients, including meat, depended on the time of year and the success of the crops. When meat was scarce, they cracked animal bones and added the bone marrow to enhance the stew's flavor.

The Penobscot also ground corn into flour to make pancakes and corn bread. The pancakes were cooked on a hot, greased stone next to the fire and sweetened with maple syrup. Corn bread was also baked on a stone next to the fire. Some of the corn bread was dried further to eat during long trips or the winter.

Clothing ➤ Traditional Penobscot clothing was made entirely from animal skins, pelts, and hides. The Penobscot painted decorations on or sewed stiff moose hair into the clothing to form patterns.

Penobscot women wore leggings that went from ankle to knee and a mid-calf-length skirt. A loose-fitting shirt that reached below their waist completed their outfit. In winter, they wore long fur robes and tall, pointed leather hats.

Penobscot men wore clothing not much different from the women. They dressed in longer leggings that came up over their thighs and attached to a belt around the waist, a *breechcloth* or a short skirt over it, and a leather shirt.

The Penobscot had lots of hats. Hunting caps helped to camouflage the hunter. Some hats had long ears attached to the top to make the wearer look like a deer or moose. Others had the wings and tail of a grouse. Feathered headdresses, made with heron, gull, or eagle feathers, were for special occasions.

THIS PICTURE TAKEN IN 1921 SHOWS A YOUNG BOY IN
TRADITIONAL PENOBSCOT CLOTHING.

Headdresses had feathers all the way around a decorative headband or just a single feather at the back.

During the warm months, the Penobscot often went barefoot. When they were not barefoot, they wore some kind of moccasins, made from deer or moose hide. The thicker moose hide was for moccasins that were worn in the woods and during the winter. Moose-hock boots, made from the skin of a moose's leg, were also used in the winter. The skin, tanned with the hair on, made the boots more waterproof than others and provided better traction on ice and snow. The Penobscot made socks from rabbit fur and wore one or more pairs under their boots.

Travel ➤ The Penobscot traveled freely throughout the Penobscot River valley and beyond. The river, its tributaries, and the lakes of the region were their main highways. The primary transportation for the Penobscot was the canoe, but they also used a system of foot trails within the hunting territories of each band. These travel routes were clearly marked for traveling in any season.

The Penobscot often had to travel in the winter to hunt and used snowshoes and toboggans to trek over the ice and snow. Their snowshoes were made from a bent ash-wood frame and a webbing of deer or moose rawhide. The Penobscot snowshoes were flat, about 4 feet (1.2 m) long and 1.5 feet (46 cm) wide. When the rivers were frozen, the Penobscot were able to pull toboggans, packed with food or firewood, by fastening a towline around their chests or foreheads.

When the rivers, streams, and lakes were free of ice, the Penobscot used canoes. Their canoes were made of white birch bark and ranged from 12 feet (3.7 m) to over 20 feet (6.1 m) long. The Penobscot were some of the most skilled canoe makers in North America and made all of their birch bark canoes in the same way.

First, they removed the bark from a large white birch tree and laid it flat on the ground. (Often the Penobscot used the same level piece of ground over and over for building bark canoes.) After laying out the piece of bark, the canoe builders carefully bent it into the shape of a finished canoe using a temporary frame in the shape of the bottom of a canoe. They placed this flat frame on the bark and added rocks to hold the frame and the bark in place. The canoe builder then slowly bent the bark up to form the sides of the canoe. Stakes would be driven into the ground to hold the bark in place until the ribs and thwarts could be added and the seams in the bark stitched.

A PENOBSCOT MAN HOLDS AN EARLY
LEATHER SNOWSHOE.

SINCE THE EARLY DAYS, THE PENOBSCOT HAVE PADDLED
CANOES ON RIVERS AND THE OCEAN. THEIR SKILL AS CANOE
BUILDERS IS WELL KNOWN.

The ribs of the canoe were thin strips of cedar that were bent in to follow the shape of the bark and give it strength. The thwarts were bars that went from side to side across the top of the canoe to hold the sides together. Any seams in the bark were stitched with spruce or cedar roots and then sealed with pitch. Finally, decorative designs were added to the top edge of the canoe. These canoes were very durable and easy to paddle and light enough to carry.

THE PENOBSCOT TODAY

At the end of the nineteenth century it looked as if the Penobscot might disappear as a tribe. At one time, they numbered as few as two hundred. According to a recent census, there are now over two thousand Penobscot. Over half of them live in Maine, and most of them still make their home on Indian Island in the Penobscot River. For many years the Penobscot were faced with the same problems of poverty, poor health, and alcoholism that have plagued many American Indian tribes.

In the 1950s, the Penobscot sought compensation for lost territory. A federal law dating all the way back to 1790 set strict guidelines for treaties between states and American Indian groups. The Penobscot and the Passamaquoddy, another Abenaki tribe in Maine, argued that a treaty signed in 1794 between the state of Massachusetts and the Penobscot violated

PRESIDENT JIMMY CARTER SIGNS THE MAINE
INDIAN CLAIMS SETTLEMENT ACT OF 1980,
AUTHORIZING A PERMANENT LAND BASE AND
TRUST FUND FOR THE LOCAL TRIBES.

this federal law. That treaty from 1794 had cost the two tribes most of their lands.

After a long court battle that started in 1970, the Penobscot and the Passamaquoddy won the largest settlement ever given to American Indians. When President Jimmy Carter signed the Maine Indian Settlement Act in 1980, the tribes were awarded $81.5 million. This award was intended to pay back the tribes for the 12,500,000 acres (5,058,500 ha) taken from them.

Of that settlement, some $54 million was used to buy back about 300,000 acres (121,400 ha). The tribes decided to invest the rest of the money in ways that would benefit their people far into the future. They bought large tracks of timberland in their original hunting territories, farmlands, and several thousand acres with development potential. Almost $3 million a year has been returned to tribal members from these investments.

A cultural resurgence has also begun. Some Penobscot are trying to relearn some of the traditional skills and lifeways that have been nearly forgotten. There is even an effort under way to create a Penobscot/English dictionary. Because of wise investments and land procurements, and a renewed sense of tradition, the Penobscot are a thriving community today.

IN AN EFFORT TO RECAPTURE SOME OF PAST PENOBSCOT
LIFE AND CULTURE, TRIBAL MEMBER CHARLES JENNINGS
CREATED THIS PAINTING IN 1989.

GLOSSARY

Agriculture The practice of growing specific plants to provide food.

Algonquian language A language with several dialects spoken by many of the original peoples of the American Northeast and East.

Artifact A man-made item that provides information about a culture.

Birch bark The bark of a white birch tree. The Penobscot used it for many things, including canoes, houses, and dishes.

Breechcloth A cloth worn to cover the midsection of the body.

Dip net A circular (or cone-shaped) net attached to a long handle that allowed the Penobscot to remove fish from their weirs.

Glooskap The creator spirit in the Penobscot's religion.

Sagamore The leader of a Penobscot band.

Shaman A religious person who was often believed to have magical powers to heal sickness and injuries.

Spawn To lay eggs (referring to fish). Some fish return to the rivers and streams of their own birth to spawn.

Tallow The hard fat deposits found in animals. American Indians and others used it to make many things, including soap and candles.

Weir An obstacle built of nets, stones, or sticks in a stream or river, which forces fish to swim through a narrow opening where they can be more easily caught.

Yard up A behavior of white-tailed deer in the winter. The deer form a herd in a growth of trees, packing down the snow and sheltering themselves from the wind. The herd feeds on the lower limbs of the nearby trees.

FOR FURTHER READING

Calloway, Colin G. *The Abenaki*. New York: Chelsea House, 1989.

———. *Indians of the Northeast*. New York: Facts on File, 1991.

Duvall, Jill. *The Penobscot*. Chicago: Childrens Press, 1993.

Norman, Howard. *How Glooskap Outwits the Ice Giants: And Other Tales of the Maritime Indians*. Boston: Little, Brown, 1989.

Utter, Jack. *American Indians: Answers to Today's Questions*. Lake Ann, Mich.: National Woodlands Publishing, 1993.

INDEX

Moose calls, 37, *38*, 39
Moose hunting, 37–39, *38*, 47

North America, 11, 12, 15, 41

Old Town, Maine, 15

Passamaquoddy Indians, 11, 54, 56
Penobscot Bay, 11, *34*
Penobscot Reservation, 11, 15
Penobscot River, 11, 12, 16, 31, 35, 49, 54
Penobscot River valley, 20
Pokeberries, 33
Population, 12, 15, 54
Poverty, 54

Rabbit family band, 18
Raven family band, 18
Religion, *17*, 20, 22–24, 37

Runners, 37

Sagamores, 20, 44
Shamans, 20, 24
Shellfish, 35, *45*, 46
Shelter, 41–44, *42*
Smallpox, 12–15
Snowshoes, *36*, 39, 49–50, *51*

Thoreau, Henry David, 16
Toboggans, 49, 50
Travel, 49–53
Treaties, 16, 20, 56
Tribal social structure, 18–20

Verrazano, Giovanni da, 12

Warfare, 15
Wildcat family band, 18
Women, *26*, *27*, 33, 35, 41, 47

ABOUT THE AUTHORS

Katherine Doherty is a librarian in a two-year technical college. Craig Doherty is an English teacher in a high school. With their daughter, Meghan, they lived on the Zuni Indian Reservation for five years, working in the Zuni Public School District. The Dohertys are also the authors of the Franklin Watts First Books *The Apaches and Navajos, The Iroquois, The Zunis,* and *The Wampanoag.* They live in New Hampshire with their daughter.